Breaking Down the Business Plan

A Business Plan for the Growth-Based Venture

Foreword

Thank you for choosing "A Business Plan for Growth-Based Ventures" as a resource for your business venture. I wrote this text to provide a straightforward guide to learning about and creating a business plan. Too many books and computer programs take readers through the steps of creating a business plan without explaining the importance of each section and how it supports the overall operations of the business. This book not only helps you create your own business plan, but also teaches you the necessary components to planning and carrying out a business.

I hope you enjoy the text. We welcome commentary and feedback on our product. Please visit our website at www.TheBusinessProfessor.com to view our other texts.

Overview of the Business Plan

Whether you have a new idea that you believe has potential or you are operating a successful business, you need a working business plan. While many businesses form and operate successfully without a business plan, developing a plan can add significant value in numerous areas of your business. This text moves step-by-step through the critical portions of the business plan. Along the way, it introduces important business management concepts and explains the significance of each section. We help you plan your business as well as teach you core business concepts that will allow you to grow and expand your business.

Purpose

The business plan has two primary purposes:

- Guiding the entrepreneur in planning individual aspects of business formation and operation, and

- Obtaining funding or capital for the business (either through bank loans or investor financing).

Our Method

As part of the planning process, we do more than simply show you how to plan your business. We teach you how to evaluate your idea or current operations and use the planning process to improve your business. After reading our text, you will be able to apply your knowledge to any business situation and add value accordingly. Our intent is to make you a stronger business professional as well as help you create or improve your business.

What to Expect

Breaking Down the Business Plan

Each chapter focuses on one component of the business plan. This is important, as each section of the business plan should be created as if it were a stand-alone document. That is to say, each component of the business plan should adequately explain, map, and allow analysis of that particular portion of the business' operations. Keeping portions of the business plan separate makes the plan a more useful and useable tool for the entrepreneur or manager.

This text goes further than simply helping you to create a business plan. We integrate critical business operations and management theory and practice into each section to help put the planning process into context. Remember, our objective is to help you plan your business and to make you a stronger business professional. In each section, we explain why the applicable material is integral to the overall successful operations of the business's. Finally, we explain what outside financiers or investors look for in each portion of the business plan.

Our Format

We focus on utility and usability. Long paragraphs can be difficult to read and use, so we use a more abbreviated format to teach business planning. Each portion of this text is short and very direct. It allows the reader to move quickly through each point and grab an overall understanding of the process. Despite the brevity, the text provides sufficient information to begin planning or, if necessary, to retrieve additional information on the topic from any other source.

Additional Resources

Visit www.TheBusinessProfessor.com for additional resources in planning, starting, and running your business.

Breaking Down the Business Plan

Overview

The business plan is a detailed roadmap for your business. It is a non-static, living, breathing document that should be updated regularly to reflect the course and strategy of the business. The business plan provides context and gives a holistic view of the entire business activity.

The business plan is both a planning tool for the entrepreneur and a tool for interacting with outside parties (particularly financiers and investors). There is no single model for a business plan. In truth, the true value of the business plan is unique to the individual entrepreneur. It allows for constant reflection on the big picture, which can become obfuscated in the daily grind of building the business.

A good business plan does not happen over night and is never complete. Remember, this is a living, breathing document that should provide a guiding light for the business at its current stage of development. As the business grows and develops, so should the business plan.

Having all of the components of your business in one place will allow you to make assessments about the process of building the business and ascertain the overall value proposition. Continue to re-think your concepts, assumptions, projections, etc. It will only help to solidify your business going forward.

Business Plan Components

The business plan will generally contain a detailed explanation of the product, service, or concept, the market, the organizational and management plan, the management team, financial position, financial projections for 3-5 years out, a marketing plan, and any other elements that would

Breaking Down the Business Plan

serve to adequately explain your business. Below we provide an overview of the individual components of the business plan.

- *The Table of Contents* - This should include the major sections of the business plan. The key is that (like a resume) you want all of the components to fit in an organized manner on one page. We use the resume analogy because the table of contents is a snapshot-style outline of the business plan. A well-planned table of contents goes a long way in showing the depth and development of the business components.

- *The Executive Summary* - This section summarizes the entirety of the business plan. It presents a concise recitation of the core function and attributes of your business. It should possess the same voice or the same tone as the body of the business plan. Often the executive summary is the only portion of a business plan that a potential investor will be willing to read. If this portion does not sufficiently explain the business objective, the value proposition to customers, and the potential for the business within the current market, the investor will discard the plan without reading any further.

- *A General Description of Your Product, Service, Idea or Concept* - As with any good plan, the strength of the plan depends entirely on how well the planner understands the initial concept. Here you will describe your product or service and the need or want that it satisfies for customers. Your product, service, or idea must create some type of value for customers. What hurt, pain, need, or want does the product or service solve. Even if the value proposition is intuitive, this section of the business plan should articulate it very well. Remember, at this point all we know is what

Breaking Down the Business Plan

the product, service, or idea is. In some cases a single product, service, or idea could be complex and have multiple value propositions that are not obvious or apparent from a general understanding of the business concept. Make sure your value proposition is stated in a manner that a CEO and your grandmother will understand.

- *Note*: The General description of the product, service, or idea should encapsulate the first 20 seconds of your "elevator pitch". If you are unfamiliar with the elevator pitch, We encourage you to research the topic on YouTube.com.

- ***A Market Analysis and Approach to Reach Customers*** - Now we move to the planning portion of the business plan. This section should outline your market analysis. This section is very broad. You can (and generally should) spend a lot of time developing this section. It includes the factors that helped you to decide to push forward with this venture or to revisit your product concept. Components in this section include: market size, segments, product or service pricing, demand, etc. We recommend doing some preliminary reading about the market analysis (visit wikipedia.com) to give you a background understanding of this process prior to beginning.

- ***Competitive (Strategic) Analysis*** - The competitive analysis is often mixed with the market analysis; however, we recommend keeping it as a separate section. The purpose of the strategic analysis is to determine your competitive position in the market (SWOT analysis, Porter's Five, or other strategic market analysis) and whether you will be able to compete. You will need to identify your primary competitors (both direct and indirect competitors)

Breaking Down the Business Plan

and explain how you will be successful in light of their presence in the market.

- **Marketing & Sales Plan** - This section outlines the methods you will use to make customers aware of your product or service. It also includes how you go about reaching and consummating sales with customers or clients. Businesses providing great products or services often fail due to a lack of sales. Marketing drives sales, but it can be extremely difficult and expensive. You will want to explain in detail the methods you will use to both spread information about your business and acquire customers or clients. This should include methods (and justifications for those methods) that are best suited to your business and within the business's budget.

- **Business Operations (A Description of How Your Business Will Carry on Activity)** - This is the "how to" section of the business plan that will explain how you are going to do what it is you do. You should give a step-by-step description of the activities that your business will undertake to deliver value to the customer. You should be detailed about your production efforts and requirements, inputs, outputs, logistics, suppliers, etc. This section can be very detailed and complicated. We definitely recommend maintaining this section as a separate, stand-alone document.

- **A Plan for how the Company will be Organized and the Management Structure** - One of the main concerns for business owners and investors is, how will the business be structured? In this section you need to explain the following: Who will be in charge of different aspects of the business and how the different functions of the business will be organized? Will there be different teams or groups that carry on

Breaking Down the Business Plan

certain functions? You will need to explain anything that involves the owners, directors, and officers, including: who will be involved in the business, what role they will play, their responsibility, their authority, the ownership rights, etc. If you plan on using outside contractors (manufacturers, consultants, programmers, accountants, attorneys, etc.) explain where their services will fit into the organization.

- ***The Financial Projections*** - This portion lays out the anticipated financial projections of the business moving forward. The financial projections generally consist of assumptions (revenues and expenses), income statement, cash flow statement, and balance sheet. Each of these documents demonstrates a different amount of information. The most important function of the financials, however, is to demonstrate the revenues and expenses (i.e., the income statement), and the flow of cash in and out of the business (i.e., the cash flow statement). Early in the business the financials will be very speculative and tenuous. A good practice is to prepare a worst case, conservative, and optimistic set of financials (particularly the income statement). You will continue to update these plans as the business develops and with every significant financial milestone.

    - Note: *Startup Expenses and Capitalization* - Generally, the breakdown of startup expenses and use of working capital is designated in the financial assumptions. This information is then employed in the income and cash flow statements. In the event you are using the plan as a tool for acquiring outside equity (Angel Investment or Venture Capital) you will need to show the proposed ownership breakdown at the anticipated capital investment rounds. Investors will be concerned about how you are

Breaking Down the Business Plan

going to use their money and what their return on revenue will be. This will necessarily include the projected ownership interest of all involved parties at different points in the life of the business.

- ***The Appendices*** - While the Financial plan is often the very last thing in the business plan, you may need to append other documents for reference. We caution against appending too many things that detract from the planning function of the overall business plan.

Learning Point

Read this section multiple times before proceeding. The overview and components of the business plan provide a snapshot of what goes into a completed business plan. You should have a holistic understanding of all plan components and the importance of each in order to fully internalize the specifics of each section. Also, understanding each section will help you identify the information that needs to be in each section and eliminate repetitive information. Now let's get started.

The Executive Summary

Overview Executive Summary

The executive summary is a summation of your entire business plan. It should tell all of the main points of the business plan in a concise format. However, there is more to writing the executive summary than simply being able to synthesize large amounts of material into a couple of short paragraphs. Many instructional guides will recommend taking the first and last sentences of each paragraph to develop the body of the summary. While this may be an effective technique for including the components of the business plan, it misses a fundamental purpose of the executive summary – creating a voice for the business. For example, if you use an exuberant and excited tone in describing your product, your executive summary should mirror this voice as well. Try to create anticipation for the body of the business plan that will follow. The business plan has to capture the essence of the business and project with the same level of exuberance, confidence, and ambition as the entrepreneur has for the business.

Aside from the voice of the Summary, translating the larger body of the business plan into a concise summary that adequately demonstrates the venture's value proposals and shares the manner in which you will deliver value is a daunting task. Your objective should be to explain the product, service, or idea, the core business model, and the value creation process to the reader in less than one page. Hopefully, after reading the executive summary, the reader will approach each section of the business plan with a basic understanding of the information contained in each section.

Drafting the Executive Summary

Most guides tell you to wait until the rest of your business plan is substantially complete before beginning work on the

Breaking Down the Business Plan

executive summary. The logic is that you cannot adequately summarize the parts of the plan until you have thought through and have begun to develop the different sections of the plan. However, we recommend a different tactic. Begin by placing a brief outline of the components of the business plan on a piece of paper. Address each section by summarizing that aspect of your product in just two sentences. For example, you have a service business that appeals specifically to the hipster market. Try to use the same level of excitement and word choice to tell how your product will be strategically positioned in the market.

You may write, "Hipsters, a market of over two million cultural standouts with a passion for iconic style preferences, are struggling to find a common marketplace to explore their artistic fashion sense without feeling that they are just supporting another commercial, clothing behemoth. Our product provides a niche alternative that customizes the web storefront to the local area, giving the boutique, non-commercial feeling that hipsters look for when paying medium-high prices for clothing, apparel, and accessories."

Notice how the above two sentences incorporate the customers need or want, the business service, and the strategic position of approaching various niche markets with medium-high cost goods. These sentences are more exciting for the reader than multiple lines of short sentences stating the value proposition, the target market, and the strategic position. Continue until you have incorporated every aspect of the business plan. Now, leave this portion and continue on with writing the individual components of the business plan. Before each section, come back to this initial executive summary. Use the excitement and passion that you put into the executive summary as a model for each section of the business plan. It will provide the inspiration and voice that you will want to carry throughout the business plan. Also, as you write the business plan, you will change, add to, and take away from the executive summary. You will see the

Breaking Down the Business Plan

body of the business plan and the executive summary mold and grow together throughout the process.

Length of the Executive Summary

Opinions vary as to the appropriate length of the executive summary. In most cases, we recommend that the executive summary be from one-half to three-quarters of a page, but no longer than one page. In truth there is no magic length for the summary. It will vary given the purpose for which you are using the summary. For example, an executive summary for a bank will generally be a bit longer than the executive summary being presented to a venture capitalist. The reason for this length disparity is a matter of time and attention to detail. A venture capitalist will want to a see a summary that concisely explains the concept – similar to the elevator pitch (business pitch). A bank lender, on the other hand, will review the plan more thoroughly as part of the business loan application. In either case, a well crafted and thorough executive summary will lay out a more complete understanding of the business that maximizes comprehension of the body of the business plan. Regardless of the length, remember that you should edit the summary to fit the intended use and expectations of the reader.

Fine Tuning the Executive Summary

Like the body of your plan, the executive summary will necessarily change and evolve as the business plan evolves. As you know you may use the business plan as either a planning tool or as a manner to obtain a loan or equity financing. We indicated above that the executive summary will also change. Regardless of whether it is strictly a planning tool for you moving forward in your business or whether you are seeking debt or equity investment, you will likely modify the executive summary slightly depending on its intended purpose.

Learning Point

In our humble opinion, the executive summary is the most valuable portion of the business plan, regardless of the plan purpose. When using the plan primarily for business planning, this section causes you to think about the business holistically. You are tasked with summarizing everything you do or plan to do into a few concise paragraphs that will appeal to intended recipient. This is where you will be able to compare the strength and fit between the portions of the business plan.

Breaking Down the Business Plan

General Company Description

Overview

In this section you will describe what your business does by laying out the details of your product, service, or idea. However, this is just the beginning. You have to describe what your business currently is (i.e., where it is in its development) and what it has the potential to be. You must also include the concept for how the business transfers value to the intended customer or client. This section of the business plan should, at a bare minimum, answer the following questions:

- What problem(s) do you plan to solve?

- What customer or client need(s) or want(s) do you hope to satisfy?

- How is your product, service, or idea interwoven into your intended markets or customer segments?

- What do you hope to accomplish or where do you hope take your business?

Give the Value Proposition

Start by telling what problem you will solve, need you will satisfy, or want you will fulfill. Before you can begin to explain your product or service and how it works, you have to lay out the value you intend to create. For example, imagine describing a stapler for the first time without first stating that you have created a revolutionary manner to clasp individual papers together without the use of bindings. You have to understand what need the stapler solves before you can go about describing the apparatus and how it functions. Remember, every product or service offered by a business satisfies a need or want of its intended customers.

Breaking Down the Business Plan

The need or want that your product or service satisfies and the manner that it satisfies it make up the value proposition to the customer.

You will also want to describe how or to what extent your product or service satisfies the customer's need or want. For example, your product may make a task easier or faster. Also, the product could be easier to use, less costly, more durable, more attractive, etc. Using the product or service could have a social impact, such as a "green" product. Choosing the type and extent of benefit(s) that your product will bestow on customers is the subject of business strategy (discussed below). As a point of caution, do not try to be all things to all people. This can cause serious problems both strategically and operationally in placing your product in the market.

Writing out the company's value proposition is a great litmus test for how well you understand your product or service and the value that it creates. If you have to hesitate and think about exactly the specific need or want that your product fulfills, then you do not have a sufficient understanding of your business. In turn, your potential customers or clients will also have difficulty in understanding the value of your product or service. It is equally a problem if your hesitation comes from the fact that your product or service could solve multiple problems or address multiple needs and wants. If you cannot concisely describe the primary benefit(s) to the main customer segment(s) (discussed in the following chapter), then your business proposition lacks focus. A lack of focus is a big problem for entrepreneurs and can derail your business planning.

- *Note*: It is important to understand how strong is the need or want among different types of customers. The strength of the need or want is generally referred to as the customer's priority. That is, how much of a priority is it for the customer to satisfy that need or

Breaking Down the Business Plan

want? The higher the priority of the product, the easier it is to convince the customer of the value proposition. In turn, higher priority generally makes the sales process easier. The only issue with high-priority, customer needs or wants is that competition with other businesses to satisfy them can be fierce.

Tell About Your Product or Service

Once you have described the product's value proposition to customers, you can go on to describe your actual product or service. Start by giving a general description of the product or service. The general description should identify the primary components of the product or major activities of the service(s) you will provide. For example, think about how you would introduce the Dyson vacuum. There are a couple of main components (internal cylinder, rotating head, etc.) of the vacuum that make it different, and potentially better, than any other vacuum on the market.

After writing a thorough description of your product or service, you can move on to introducing a technical description of your product or a detailed statement of how you will deliver your service. Break down the product or service into its individual components. If there are several pieces to a product or it has multiple mechanical functions, then you will need to describe each component that is important to creating the customer value. If your service business involves multiple services (even if the services are related), you should describe in detail each value-creating service performed. With a service you will want to focus on the outcomes of each service and, if applicable, how it fits into a greater customer need.

- *Note*: It may be the case that the workings of the product or service are complicated. If your product involves patents or technical diagrams you may want to make reference to them in this section and append

Breaking Down the Business Plan

them to the end of the business plan. This is particularly true with cloud-based software (SAAS) or detailed service models. If you have a complicated service delivery model, we recommend leading off with a flowchart, diagram, process matrix, infographic, or some other demonstrative tool to show an overview of all of the working components. There are lots of programs on the market that make developing interesting forms of graphic media very easy.

Outline the Basic Strategic Position of the Business

Once you have your product's value proposition and a description of its function, you can now begin to explain how your product or service will be able to compete or address the problem, need, or want better than the alternatives that exist. You will address the full strategic (competitive) analysis later in the business plan. In this section, you want to lend support to your value proposition by expressing what your product or service does and how it does it better or differently than those already in the industry. That is, "what is your product's competitive strategy?"

What do we mean by focus on a competitive strategy?

Types of competitive strategies generally include:

- cost strategies (low cost structure),

- product or service differentiation strategies (uniqueness of your product or service), and

- focus strategies (cost or differentiation strategy in niche or isolated markets).

For example, you may want to pursue a cost strategy (i.e., you have an advantage in your customer pricing because of

Breaking Down the Business Plan

the low cost structure of your product or service). In this case, you will describe how your product will leverage the low cost structure to gain a competitive advantage over competitors. This could include a lower price point for customers, a high margin at average industry prices, or a super-high margin at above-average, industry pricing. Note, at average or above-average industry pricing, you will need another competitive advantage to attract customers to your product above those of competitor.

Another example of a strategic position is to differentiate your product or service. Let's use our vacuum example above. Dyson sells a $600 vacuum. This price point is well above the industry average for a vacuum. Dyson, however, differentiates its product to customers in order to create its value proposition. Dyson's strategic position is the higher-powered motor and unique mechanisms in the head for picking up dirt and debris. Restated, for customers or clients who are not as cost-sensitive, the differentiating factor is increased performance in multiple mechanical functions. A product or service can be differentiated from other products or services in the market in a number of ways. A good exercise for understanding competitive strategy is to look at multiple brands of products on a shelf. What characteristic of each product does the manufacturer tout on the packaging?

- *Note*: Later, in the competitive analysis portion of the business plan, you will address the major players and competitors who control parts of the market. There you will also explain your competitive strategy as a comparison to their products or services. For more information on business strategy, we encourage you to do some independent reading on Porter's Generic Strategies.)

Incorporate Your Company Goals and Missions Statement

Breaking Down the Business Plan

The best way to understand where you are in your business is to compare your current position with where you want to be. When you are a business intended on growing you must have a clear path of where you want to go. Later in the business plan, you will identify your specific milestones for growth and your financial projections for the future. In the general business description section you want to focus more on the overall outcome you desire for your business. This could mean developing a stable lifestyle business that supports you for years to come (known as a "lifestyle business") or, in the alternative, it could mean that you want to achieve rapid growth and sell the business within a few years ("startup venture"). Either way, writing out your company goals will help you stay on track as the business develops and will allow third parties to understand your business's path.

Many businesses identify their objective in a mission statement. The mission statement is a concise statement of the company's goals and the principles that will guide its growth. Many people see the business's mission statement as more symbolic than practical. However, the mission statement can serve a very practical purpose in providing a path for a growing and evolving business. Start by asking yourself the following questions:

- What value does my business create for the customer?

- What value does the company provide for the owners and team members?

- How do we intend to develop or change that value proposition over time?

- How do we incorporate those intended changes into business operations?

Breaking Down the Business Plan

Focusing on the value that your business creates for the customer will help you focus on how the business's goals match up against those of the customer. If the value to your customer is the uniqueness that they feel by using your niche product, then a goal of expanding to a broader market may not fit with your customer's goals.

The value proposition to customers and the business will naturally change as a business develops and grows. New customer segments will spring up, and companies will adopt secondary goals (e.g., growth milestones, profitability, community impact, innovation, etc.). If you understand your goals early, you can plan for how to implement these goals into the operational aspects of the business. That is, you will understand the need to either expand operations and grow personnel or enter into new markets and geographies where your goals can create the desired customer and business value.

You may wish to expand this section further to include a business philosophy. Is your business guided by principle or belief? If so, without incorporating the business' philosophy directly into the planning documents it may become difficult to incorporate and maintain those principles as the business grows and evolves.

Learning Point

In this section you have laid the foundation for what the company does and how it will create and transmit value to the client or customer. The parts of the business plan that follow will add greater explanation to how this value creation is possible, will be carried out, and what the results of the venture will be.

The Market Analysis

Overview

Please read this section carefully. The market analysis is the backbone of a well-developed business plan. The market analysis serves two functions:

- learning about your business market, and

- demonstrating your understanding of how your product or service will fit within the subject market.

Learning about the market provides the information necessary to determine whether a product, service, or idea is a valid business opportunity. In this context, it is often called the feasibility analysis or study. This is a very important undertaking for any entrepreneur. The process should be in-depth and include lots of primary and secondary market research. You will use the information you uncover to build the subsequent sections of the business plan, such as the financial projections.

Conducting a thorough market analysis is easily the subject matter of an entire text. In this book we line out the primary information that you will need to develop and include in the market analysis portion of the business plan. While this information is critical, it should only be a fraction of the research that an entrepreneur undertakes prior to undertaking a new business or startup venture.

Understanding the Market

The first stage of conducting a market analysis is to develop a plan for conducting research about the market. Market research is generally split into two types:

- primary research, and

- secondary research.

Secondary research involves using material prepared by third parties that may or may not be specifically oriented to your market. Basically, it involves identifying information uncovered by others (such as research groups, the Government, industry experts, etc.) that is relevant to your business. Common examples of secondary market research includes looking to population and demographic data taken by the government, consumer surveys, targeted articles or surveys, or data derived from other studies.

- *Example*: You may access the county census records to determine how many people live in an area, their age groups, how many people live in the average home, etc. You can use this information to target sales and marketing efforts to localities made up of your target market demographic. This information will allow you to maximize the return on your marketing and sales expenditures.

Primary research, on the other hand, involves direct research of your intended customers. Direct research of customers generally involves some form of informational gathering about the customer's preferences, such as questionnaires, or surveys. It could also include observational research, such as the monitoring of potential customers to determine preferences or characteristics of their consumption or purchasing activity.

- *Example:* A good example of direct research regards the use of customer loyalty cards at any grocery store. Grocery stores issue customer value cards to customers who swipe those cards in order to receive discounts at the time of purchase. The customer enjoys the value of lower priced groceries, while the grocery store records your grocery purchase habits.

Breaking Down the Business Plan

Assuming that you use the card each time that you grocery shop, the store knows what you purchase, how often you purchase items, and a host of other information about your grocery spending habits. The grocery store will use this information to better understand the customer base and to develop targeted marketing plans. To effectively collect and use large amounts of customer information or data, it helps to have a strong handle on statistical analysis. Statistical analysis allows you to make sense out of the many characteristics you identify in your customers and understand how they correlate to characteristics of the overall market. We strongly encourage you to undertake outside reading on how statistical methods can be used to analyze a business market.

Primary and secondary research will produce two types of information about your potential customers:

- qualitative information, and

- quantitative information.

Qualitative information is any non-numerical information about the market. This could be information about trends or general demographic about your customer segment(s). For example, knowing that a certain item or product is becoming fashionable or has a strong reputation among teenage females is qualitative information.

Quantitative information includes quantities or other numerical information. For example, quantitative data would include the number of certain individuals (such as teenage females) in a specific geographic region.

From these examples you can see how quantitative and qualitative information combine to provide relevant information about the market. This information will be

Breaking Down the Business Plan

instrumental in evaluating the business opportunity and scoping your approach to conducting business.

Once you have a strong understanding of the characteristics of individuals in your surrounding markets, you need to determine how your product or service fits in the relevant markets and what are the characteristics of the individuals who will purchase your product or service.

Outline the Product or Service Characteristics

This section focuses on your understanding your product. Start be creating on or two line answers for the following questions:

- What are the primary features and attributes of your products?

- How will your customer perceive your product?

The point in answering these questions is to characterize your product from the viewpoint of the potential consumer. As the entrepreneur you naturally have a bias or preconceived notion as to the value of your product or service and how it will be received by your potential customers. Examining the product or service from the customer's point of view will help you to be objective and unbiased in describing your product or service's attributes and benefits to the customer.

Some product or service attributes will be valued by one potential customer, but not by another. This information allows you to identify your target markets (discussed below). Further, some attributes may be obvious to customers, while other attributes are not. If you discover or determine that some of the attributes or benefits are not intuitive in the product or service (i.e., they are not obvious or readily ascertainable), you will want to begin scoping a plan on how

Breaking Down the Business Plan

you will make your potential customer aware of these attributes or benefits. This will be very important later as you draft the Marketing Plan section.

Identify the Target Market(s) and Customer Segment(s)

You understand your product and how the general population will see your product or service. Now you must identify the individuals who or businesses that are potential customers. Remember, your product or service will necessarily solve a problem or satisfy a need or want for the customer. Ask yourself these questions.

- What needs or wants does my product fulfill or alleviate?

- What types of customers have this need, hurt, or want?

A customer segment is the grouping of particular types of customers together. Customers have different needs or wants, and your product or service may satisfy different needs or wants for the same or different customers. If you are able to identify a specific need or want that your product or service satisfies for a large number of customers, a detailed market analysis will help you to identify the information about those customers and fit them into groups with like customers. These potential customer groups are now a customer segment.

Once you identify your customer segments, you will want to include the following information about each customer segment:

- Identifying characteristics of the segment
    - The type of need or want satisfied

Breaking Down the Business Plan

- - The uniform demographic characteristics of the segment

- Size of the customer segment
    - \# of total customers
    - Total value expended by these customers on this need or want within a given time period.

- Level of priority of each customer segment for the product
    - Level or strength of desire for the product or service
    - Average quantity of product or service purchased at a time).

The type of need or want may include: sustenance, obligations (social, moral, financial, or legal), efficiency, or entertainment.

Demographic characteristics of your potential individual customers (i.e., customer demographics) include: age, race, sex, ethnicity, geographic location, Income level, socio-economic status, family background, political or religious beliefs, memberships and organizations, level of education, etc.

Demographic characteristics of your potential business customers include: industry, size (products, employees, locations), revenue, ownership structure, market capitalization, competitive status in the market, geographic locations, growth rate, strategic plans (cost, differentiation, focus), and any other potentially relevant information that identifies or quantifies the level of demand (want or need).

Breaking Down the Business Plan

Note: We encourage you to undertake additional reading and study to learn more about identifiable market demographics.

Determine Your Primary & Secondary Target Market(s)

Ok, we have analyzed our product objectively and figured out what features and benefits will interest certain customers. We have divided those customer groups into segments based on their characteristics. Now, you will need to prioritize the amount of demand each customer segment has for the product or service. That is, how urgent is the need or want you will fulfill? With this information you will be able to deduce the most valuable segment or the segment that has the capability of producing the greatest amount of profit for your business. This will be your primary target market. Other customer segments that produce lesser value will be secondary markets.

The relevant question that you are trying to identify for each potential customer segment is: "Will it produce a net benefit (i.e., be profitable) to market my product to any particular segment?" In some cases it may be too difficult or too expensive to adequately capitalize on targeting a particular market. There could be marketing, sales, logistics, operational, or strategic costs that make reaching a certain market segment unrealistic or unprofitable. If a market segment is not sufficiently large or the sales margin sufficiently high, you will focus your resources on meeting the needs or wants of and specifically marketing to the more profitable segment. As such, you will want to have a firm handle on the feasibility of certain market segments.

Below are some of the questions you will want to ask in determining your target market.

- Given my available resources, which market segments can I feasibly reach?

Breaking Down the Business Plan

- What is the size of each feasible market segment?

- Is one existing market segment prone to more growth than another? (i.e., Is one market segment growing?)

- Is demand within the market segment created by a unique need or a want?

  - *Note*: Be cautious in assuming that your product, service, or idea will create demand that previously did not exist. Few businesses offer something that creates a previously non-existent demand in the market.

- What is the strength of demand within each market segment?

  - *Note*: Some market segments have strong seasonal demand or demand is strong because of an existing trend. You will need to account for this possibility.

- What is the urgency (priority) of demand within each market segment?

  - *Note*: This will be very important in selecting the most profitable market segment, as a high degree of priority reduces the need to expend more effort and funds on marketing to the individual segment.

- Is there any strategic information that could be relevant to entering the market at this time?

  - *Note*: This usually includes market trends or major changes within the market.

Breaking Down the Business Plan

- What percentage of each market segment can I realistically capture?

    - *Note*: Remember to be conservative in your assessment. Sometime capturing even 1% of a total market share is not realistic. You may need to break the market segment down to immediate geographical areas in order to arrive at a realistic percentage.

- What is the price point for each market segment?

    - *Note*: There are a number of ways to determine how much each market segment will pay for the product using primary and secondary research.

- What price point should I set that captures the highest percentage or the most profitable combination of each market segment?

    - *Note*: This is a strategic consideration that you should justify when determining your price point. If you price your product to appeal to a smaller segment of high-end users because of the higher profit margin, you may alienate a large percentage of another market segment. The trick is to determine at what price point you will reach the most profitable mix of potential customers.

- Given the feasibility, urgency, and price point, how should I prioritize my marketing efforts?

    - *Note*: You will undoubtedly have to prioritize your marketing efforts. Given the high cost of marketing and the scarcity of resources for new businesses, the lion's share of marketing efforts will revolve around your primary target market.

Breaking Down the Business Plan

In the early stages of your business, you will generally only devote minimal effort to attracting secondary market segments. Understanding the profitability factors will help you understand where to focus these efforts.

Do your best to include answers to all of these questions in your market analysis. Provide the primary and secondary research that supports your conclusions for each section. If you use secondary resources, it may be a good idea to append the relevant provision to the end of the business plan. If you conduct primary research, you may want to explain the methods you used and append any questionnaires or surveys to the end of the business plan.

Learning Point

Remember that your business plan has multiple potential purposes (planning, satisfying lenders, attracting investors). The market analysis portion demonstrates that you understand your market. You have identified the potential profitable market segments and have a plan for addressing those profitable portions of the market. Your primary and secondary research will give you the information that you need to make decisions and justify your position. Other portions of the business plan, such as the marketing plan and financial projections will build upon the information that you include in the market analysis section (e.g., such as product pricing). Devoting considerable time to this portion will help you to focus on customers that offer the greatest value proposition for the business.

Competitive Analysis

Overview

In this section you will identify the competitive landscape, your competitors, and your strategy for competing in your product or service industry.

When conducting your initial market analysis, you acquired information necessary to determine whether the market will allow your business to produce the desired type and amount of value. This begs the question, "why, if the market has the ability to create value for new businesses, do more businesses not enter that particular market?"

The answer to this question is the subject of the competitive analysis portion of the business plan. In any market there are certain factors that prevent or discourage other producers or providers from entering the market. These are commonly known as "barriers to entry". Barriers to entry may include cost of entry, cost of operations, competitive landscape, etc. An entrepreneur who is uncertain about her ability to overcome these barriers may decide not to enter and compete in a given market.

The significance of competition in the market is best understood through simple, economic principles.

An Economic Outlook: Supply and Demand

In any market there is a certain level of supply and demand for a given product or service. Individuals demand a certain amount of a product or service at any given price. Generally, the lower the price the higher the demand. As the price rises, the demand goes down. Producers or providers of goods and services will produce a certain amount of goods at a given price. At high prices (which will produce higher profits if the costs associated with production are uniform)

Breaking Down the Business Plan

businesses will produce more of the product to claim the available value. As long as there is value to be had, new firms will continue to enter the market. These new entrants will invariably compete against other firms by lowering prices. This increases the overall amount of demand, because the price is lower. However, this also reduces the value (or profit) available to the businesses. As such, fewer businesses will be able to enter and compete in the market. In turn, the market becomes more competitive, and only the larger businesses who can use economies of scale to lower their production costs will be able to compete. The benefit goes to the customer, as the larger business produces the greatest amount of goods at the lowest price for consumers.

The economic characteristics of an industry are crucial factors in business decision-making. Competition and the number of suppliers in the market drive the supply of a given product. Entering a saturated market with over supply of a product or service and low price point can cause a business to fail to produce the type and amount of desired value. Likewise, a market with very strong competitors can be treacherous for a new business. Below we provide an overview of some of the tools used to determine the opportunities available for a business in a given market.

Tools of the Trade

Now that you understand the economics of market competition, it's time to explain the competitive landscape within your business plan. There are a number of accepted models for understanding your place within a competitive market. One of the most commonly utilized is the SWOT Analysis. SWOT stands for strengths, weaknesses, opportunities, and threats. This analysis allows a business to self-assess and identify both the opportunities that exist and the threats to avoid when competing in the market.

The value of the *SWOT analysis* is as follows:

Breaking Down the Business Plan

- *Strengths*

    - What strengths are inherent in your business, plan, or team?

    - How do these strengths make you more competitive in the market or industry?

    - How do these strengths compare to the strengths of competitors in the market?

- *Weaknesses*

    - What visible, internal weaknesses can you see in the business?

    - How will these weaknesses make you less competitive in the market?

    - How do these weaknesses compare to those of competitors in the market?

- *Opportunities*

    - What opportunities are evident from the current market situation?

    - Why do these opportunities exist?

    - How will you be able to take advantage of these opportunities?

- *Threats*

    - What internal (inside the business) threats exist to you accomplishing your business goals?

Breaking Down the Business Plan

- What external threats exist that could derail your business plans?

- Are these threats unique to you, or are they generally present in the industry?

The SWOT analysis is the most widely employed tool for assessing one's competitive position in the market, but it is just a piece of the overall competitive puzzle.

Another common strategic assessment tool is known as *Porter's 5 Forces*. This construct was developed by the famed Harvard professor, Michael Porter and is a staple in general business strategy. Porter examined the competitive landscape based on five forces that determine the strength or power of a business within the market.

- *Supplier Power*: Supplier power addresses the relative strength of suppliers in the industry. A supplier with high power has a greater ability to bargain for and capture value in the exchange of value between them and the customer (your business). That is, the higher the supplier power the more control she has over prices (ability to drive up costs) for the business. If your business is not capable of passing the costs along to customers, then it lowers your profit margin and your competitive position in the market. Don't think of the supplier analysis as examining a single supplier; rather, it involves the entire group of suppliers in the market. Supplier power is generally a product of the number of factors including the following:

    - the number of suppliers in the market,

    - the value proposition of any supplier's goods,

Breaking Down the Business Plan

- competitive advantage to any individual suppliers,

- lack of substitute products on the market,

- the cost of switching to a different supplier,

- diversification of the suppliers, and

- threat of supplier integration.

- **Buyer Power**: Buyer power regards the ability of customers to control product prices in your market. Customers are powerful when they are able to grab more value in an exchange by either driving up costs or demanding higher quality or quantity of service or product at a given price. Buyer power is important for both B2B (business-to-business) and B2C (business-to-customer) businesses. Here are some situations in which buyers possess greater power to control prices:

  - number of buyers,

  - important individual customers,

  - low cost of switching, and

  - price sensitivity of the buyer.

- **Competitive Rivalry**: Competitive rivalry concerns the ability of your competitors to increase their market share. If you have numerous competitors or any competitors with superior value propositions (lower price, higher quality product, etc.) then your competitors have strong market power. Below are some common scenarios where competitors have high levels of market power:

Breaking Down the Business Plan

- a large number of competitors in the market,
- competition through price, and
- competition through differentiation.

- **Threat of Substitutes**: The threat of substitutes or substitution regards the ability of other (non-industry) products or services to meet the wants or needs of your customer base. It also concerns the ability and motivation of customers to figure out a way to fulfill the need or want without your product or service. If this is possible, then it weakens your business' market power by placing limits on prices of your product or service.

- **Threat of New Entry**: This concerns the ability of new competitors to enter the market. As we discussed above, new competitors entering the market increases competition and ultimately pushes down prices. Further, new competitors will occupy some portion of the market which may diminish your business's existing market share. So, the ability of new competitors to enter the market easily indicates lower market power.

Porter's five forces are very useful for understanding where an established business sits within the market. However, it is also very useful to the startup to assess the competitiveness of a particular industry.

What to Include in the Business Plan

The two tools above are very good at producing information that is relevant to your business planning. Now, depending on your business objectives, you need to determine what information to include in the business plan.

Breaking Down the Business Plan

All of the information uncovered during the market analysis and noted during the competitive analysis is relevant and useful to planning your business. Some information, however, will be particularly important to lenders to show that you have adequately planned the business. Other information will be more important to equity investors who want to assess your business's probability of success. While it is not wrong to include more information than necessary, it can cause the business plan to be overly voluminous and difficult to use. Below are some recommendations to overcome this issue.

When drafting the competitive analysis portion of the plan, at a bare minimum, you should answer the following questions:

- Why are others (competitors) entering or not entering the market?

    ▫ Note: This question asks you to provide the barriers or hurdles that exist when trying to get into the business.

- Why will you be able to enter and compete in the market?

    ▫ Note: If you are entering the market (where others are not), what will allow you to overcome these barriers to entry?

- How will you be successful in expanding the market or winning the market share of other competitors?

    ▫ Note: Once in the market, you will face many competitors. What competitive advantage(s) do you have that will allow you to be successful?

Breaking Down the Business Plan

Taking a Look at Competitive Factors

What are your barriers to entry? Assuming that you are not yet in the market, what is it going to take to get there? This will generally be the reason or explanation why others are not in the market. Remember, the chances are not good that you are the first person or business to come up with an idea for a product or service. In that case, there must be something that is keeping others out. This may not be obvious at first, but identifying these early will allow you to make adjustments to meet and overcome these hurdles.

Start the competitive analysis section by identifying the barriers to entry and explain how they may effect your business or industry. After each barrier, explain how you intend to overcome it. Below are examples of common barriers to entry and some questions to help you address the issue in your particular situation:

- Funding or Capital Concerns

    - How much capital is required up front?

    - Will it require some level of revolving capital needs?

    - Where are you going to get this capital?

- Legal Barriers (Licensing, Regulatory Approval)

    - Is there a required state or federal license?

    - Does the product or service require inspection and approval by a state or federal regulatory agency?

Breaking Down the Business Plan

- Is the business subject to some state or federal regulation that is subject to change? (e.g., labor laws, foreign embargoes, etc.)

- Costs of Production

    - Is there a cost of production that is inhibitive in starting out?

    - What is the cost structure for competitors?

    - Does any competitor have a clear cost advantage? If so, how? Why?

    - How will you overcome this cost of production barrier?

- Cost of Sales and Marketing

    - What is the industry cost structure for sales and marketing?

    - Are there any competitors that have a clear advantage in this cost structure? If so, how?

    - How do you plan to address this barrier?

- Logistical Concerns

    - How are you going get your raw material or other supplies for conducting business?

    - How are you going to deliver your goods or services to your customers?

    - Will it involve outsourcing or international shipping?

Breaking Down the Business Plan

- Will this require strategic presence or distribution centers in various locations?

- *Note*: You should brainstorm how each aspect of the business that requires the movement of product or material from one place to another will take place. Much of this information can be gleaned from competitors or businesses with similar business models. Understanding the logistical concerns will allow you to estimate costs and budgeting. Further, you may uncover a logistical aspect that supplies a competitive advantage to another business or, potentially, your planned business.

- Required Skills and Knowledge

    - Who are you going to need to involve to carry out your business?

    - How does your business team's skill level compare to that of competitors?

    - *Note*: It is a common mistake for the entrepreneur to believe that she can personally carry on too many of the actual business functions. If you have not realized, you will be preoccupied with countless tasks and will not be able to carry on many of the tasks that you now assume will be your responsibility. You need to have an understanding of what you do not have the time or ability to do. Again, look to competitors or similar businesses to determine the skills or market knowledge necessary to carry on your planned business operations.

- Employee Concerns

Breaking Down the Business Plan

- □ Can you find employees with the skill and availability to fulfill the needs of the business?

- □ Will you be able to meet the employee benefit requirements, such as health insurance, unionized demands, etc.?

- □ *Note*: Employee concerns are countless and daunting. There is no way to project the types of employee troubles that you may face in starting your business. Examples of employee issues include: hiring, training, employee benefits (compensation, healthcare, retirement), union negotiations, lawsuits (discrimination or hostile environment), and firing. The employee concerns for which you can plan include: hiring, training, and employee benefits. All of these issues can entail considerable costs that were not previously anticipated. Planning and buying insurance for unplanned legal events can help to minimize these issues.

- Intellectual Property

  - □ How are you going to protect your process or product?

  - □ Does your product or service involve or potentially infringe on the intellectual property rights of others?

  - □ *Note*: Generally, the only way to protect your intellectual property is through patent, trademark, copyright, or trade secret. Some businesses develop around a product or service with the idea that they can start up under the radar of competitors and then grow quickly before competitors can catch up. This is commonly referred to as, "running faster" than the competition. In general, this is a last resort strategy, as outrunning a competitor with superior funding is very difficult. Start by looking at the nature of your product or service and try to determine the best way to protect or establish defendable ownership or intellectual property rights.

- Taxation

    - What will be the applicable taxes and tax rates?

    - Are there any tax advantages that exist for carrying on your business?

    - What tax advantages are your competitors employing that allow them to carry on business in an otherwise unprofitable venture?

    - *Note*: There may be economic development or energy savings associated with your business venture. Also you may need legal assistance to identify the effect of choosing a particular business entity above another. Again, a percentage of tax savings can make a considerable difference in profit margin or overall profitability of your business.

- Strong (Large) Competitors

    - How strong are the competitors?

    - What tactics are they likely to employ to defeat your product or service or to keep you from stealing market share?

Breaking Down the Business Plan

- *Note*: A large, well-capitalized competitor may be able to engage in a price war that you cannot withstand. This will require both primary and secondary research of your actual and potential competitors. (This concept is developed further below.)

You may not include all of the above-listed competitive barriers within the business plan; however, they are important considerations when planning your business. For any of the above entry barriers, you should explain how you will deal with the current situation, the situations that will arise along your projected growth path, and any contingent changes in these factors that could affect your business.

Competitor Analysis

After identifying the general barriers to getting into the industry or market and how you will overcome them, you should indicate the level of competition that you expect to face. Start by preparing an extensive list of the players who will compete against you in your immediately relevant and prospective markets. Then take the following steps to analyze their market position and strength.

- List each competitor name, location, and give a brief profile of his or her product or service.

- Create sub-categories and groupings for the competitors who are your most direct competitors.

- Indicate the relative strength of the competitors.
    - You will list aspects such as:
        - Percentage of market held

Breaking Down the Business Plan

- Market capitalization
- Annual revenue
- Brand recognition
- Competitive or innovative nature of firm
- Strategic relationships (such as with suppliers, manufacturers, distribution network, marketers, etc.)

- *Note*: This list is by no means exhaustive. You should attempt to indicate any characteristic, quality, position, relationship, etc., that provides a strength or benefit to the business.

- Expand on the secondary or indirect competitors.

  - Give and explanation of why you believe their product or service is a competitor to yours. This could explain how their product or service is a substitute product.

  - Explain the situation in which these secondary or indirect competitors would be the greatest threat to your projected business. For example, if a competitor offers an inferior good (product or service), a downturn in the economy may drive customers away from your more economically *elastic* product. We encourage you to conduct outside research on the concept of elasticity of demand.

- Explain how your product or service is superior (or competitively advantaged) to each competitor's product or service.

Breaking Down the Business Plan

- ▫ The most difficult part of this component is identifying all of the characteristics that customers covet in the product or service, such as: design, speed, ease of use, dependability, price, customer service, etc.

- ▫ It may be useful to use a table listing the attributes of the products side-by-side. This allows for quick assessment by third parties, and it provides a framework for you to conceptualize the market position of your product or service. You can create multiple tables comparing your product or service to each category or individual competitor. You will need to customize the lists of competitive factors for each competitor or competitor's product. Note: These individual tables may not fit within the body of the business plan. You can always append or attach them to the appendices.

Learning Point

Developing the competitive analysis section requires a great deal of research and knowledge about other business's products or services. The most difficult portion is assessing your business's strengths and weaknesses. It is important to be as honest and objective as possible in analyzing your value proposition. It may be useful to enlist third parties who are unbiased or unrelated to your business to provide their opinion on your product. This will help you to avoid the cognitive bias that nearly all entrepreneurs have when assessing the competitive strengths of their own products or services. Remember, even if you can explain away any fears or negative perceptions that customers have about your product, customer input is extremely valuable. Remember, you will not be there to explain away these fears or concerns at the point in which the customer learns of the product.

Breaking Down the Business Plan

These will be the perception issues that you have to address in marketing your product or service.

The Marketing Plan

In prior sections, you analyzed the market for your product or service and identified a strategic plan for targeting customers. The marketing plan section regards building a marketing and sales plan ("marketing plan") for your business. The marketing plan is broken into a promotion section and a sales section. The promotion section involves how you will disperse information to make potential customers aware of your product or service. The sales portion of the marketing plan outlines how you will consummate sales transactions with your client or customer.

- *Note*: Creating an effective marketing plan requires using the information acquired in the market and competitive analysis.

Below we review the information already acquired and necessary for writing the marketing plan. Then we move into assembling the plan.

Understanding Your Market

Understanding one's place in the market is not as easy as it sounds. It requires an in-depth understanding of your product or service, your customers, and how your customers perceive your product or service. The following questions should help you understand what makes your product or service unique in the eyes of your prospective customer.

- How do you see your product or service?

- How do you see your product or service being used by customers?

- Who do you see as your primary customers?

Breaking Down the Business Plan

- Do you have any secondary customers? If so, who are they?

- What function is your product or service serving for customers?

- Why is this customer using my product or service, as apposed to another product or service?

Once you fully explore the above questions, you should look to third parties for their opinions. As entrepreneurs we are inevitably influenced by our own perception biases. When seeking the input of third parties, do not focus solely on the individuals who you see as your target market. Get feedback from non-target-market individuals as well. This will help you to expand your understanding of how your product is perceived by a variety of individuals in the market.

Marketing Strategy

Once you feel that you fully understand your market, you can begin outlining a marketing strategy. Marketing strategy, by definition, regards how you will employ certain tools and tactics to reach your customers. Many people confuse strategy with tactics. Tactics are measures, tools, or techniques employed to carry out a function. Strategy, on the other hand, involves a holistic approach regarding how you will address the market. The dominant tool for developing a general business strategy was proposed by Michael Porter in 1985 and is known as Porter's Generic Strategies. As mentioned in the General Company Description section, Porter proposed that any strategy is a subset of three main strategies:

- *Cost* - This regards the cost structure to firms. The ability to set one's price is limited by the costs of producing the product or service. For example, a decision to pursue a low price, high volume strategy is limited by the total costs of production. The decision to be a luxury good generally requires higher costs and price.

- *Differentiation* - A differentiation strategy regards providing a unique product or service. That is, there is something about the product or service that differentiates it from other competitors' products or services. Offering features that are not available elsewhere is an example of differentiation strategy.

- *Focus* - A focus strategy means to concentrate the business' efforts in niche or isolated markets. For example, focusing on a smaller niche market will often allow a business to operate free from competition from major competitors in the industry. A focus strategy can include a cost focus or differentiation focus within the target market.

These general strategies are subject to further development by each individual firm.

Developing the Plan

The Product Message

It is important to have a section that adequately summarizes your intended product message. Your product message combines your marketing strategy and the value proposition that you hope to transmit to your customers. Think of your product or service image and the brand that you want to build for your product or service. Associate it with a marketing strategy. Do you want to be seen as the most innovative, the most affordable, the highest quality, the fastest, the easiest to use, etc.? Unfortunately, your product cannot be all things to all people. Concentrate on the primary and secondary customers that you hope to reach.

Breaking Down the Business Plan

You will develop a general strategy that has necessary modification for each potential type of customer.

- *Example*: If you understand your product and your customer, you will craft your product message(s) to support your product or service to those individuals. You may use an environmentally friendly, product message to reach young environmentally conscious customers. On the other hand, you may use product quality and ease of use to reach older, affluent customers.

Be careful in developing multiple product messages. This can dilute your message and make your desired brand seem manufactured or disingenuous. Remember, there is no single guide for who is your customer and what that customer wants from your product. You will better understand your customer by fully understanding your product and your market. Once you have these base understandings, you can employ the available tools and tactics required to deliver that message.

Promotion

In this section, you will outline the individual components of your promotion plan. Promotion involves how you reach your customers with your product or service message. Promotion includes your advertising plan and the channels of communication you will use. Below are categories of marketing tools to employ in communicating your message.

- *Traditional Marketing Tools*: Setting up at trade shows, catalogs ads, television, radio, newspaper, yellow pages, signs or billboards, direct mail, brochure distribution, sales representatives or agents, placing your product with retailers, word of mouth marketing.

Breaking Down the Business Plan

- *Emerging Marketing Tools*: Pay-per-click advertising (Google, Bing, Yahoo, Facebook), website development and search engine optimization (SEO), sales sites (amazon or professional service listing sites), non-traditional sales force models (e.g., Salesforce.com), direct email marketing (e.g., mailchimp.com), and social media marketing (Twitter, Facebook, etc.), etc.

The promotion method you employ should depend on whether your customers are more likely to find you *via* traditional or new advertising methods. Perhaps, given your available marketing budget, you will use a hybrid of these approaches in order to maximize your reach. Remember, there will be different costs associated with each type of advertising.

Sales Distribution Channels

This section should describe how you are going to physically transfer value between you and the customers or clients. That is, what channel will you use to provide your product or service to the customer? Remember, this decision should be consistent with your overall marketing strategy.

Developing a sales model is a broad topic and the subject of a stand-alone text. Common methods of delivery include the following:

- employing internal or external sales agents or representatives,

- selling through wholesalers,
    - e.g., placement in small retail stores,
    - e.g., selling through big-box retailers,

Breaking Down the Business Plan

- establishing sales facilities (stores) in strategic locations,

- selling through sales catalogs and magazines, and

- selling through first-party and third-party websites.

As you can see, your distribution plan may involve multiple channels. To determine an effective sales model for your business, we recommend studying the sales models employed by competitors and similar product or service businesses. This type of primary or secondary research can help you avoid making costly and time-consuming errors when planning your sales efforts.

As with your marketing efforts, you will want to employ a sales plan that maximizes the sales you achieve per dollar spent. As your business revenue goes up, you will begin employing less efficient sales channels in order to reach additional customers (secondary markets).

Prices

What price will you charge for your product? As part of your marketing strategy, you will determine whether your product or service is the highest quality, lowest price, easiest to use, etc. Whichever of these competitive strategies you hope to achieve and promote, you will need to price the product accordingly.

Your first step in determining the product or service price is to determine the price customers are willing to pay for the product or service. Consistent with principles of supply and demand, as the price for a product goes up fewer customers will be willing to buy the product or service. Your role is to determine the combination of sales volume and price that will maximize your profit. This could mean serving fewer

Breaking Down the Business Plan

customers at a higher price or serving more customers at a lower price.

Determining what a customer is willing to pay often involves both primary and secondary research. Primary research will involve using questionnaires and surveys among potential or target customers to determine what they believe the price of the product would or should be. Secondary research will involve looking up the prices of similar products or services already in the market. Researching competitor prices will provide a general guide for your customers' price range. Alternatively, using customer surveys or questionnaires is often the most effective manner of determining a particular market segment's willingness to pay.

When drafting the marketing portion of the business plan, you will want to explain how you arrived at your product price. This information will be valuable for third parties. Using the hard statistics from your primary and secondary research will help satisfy the inquiries of future equity investors who question your pricing. Further, you will want to explain how this price fits in your overall marketing strategy (i.e., you charge higher prices because are trying to be the luxury provider).

Sales Forecast

Now that you have a marketing plan, including the intended product or service price, you can begin projecting your sales. Your sales revenue will depend upon your volume of sales at a given price. As your business grows, you will be able to expand to additional markets and reach other customer segments. You will be able to use your sales forecast to project your rate of growth and expected future revenue and expenses.

Begin by developing a sales worksheet where you outline your monthly projected sales. Like your price, your sales

Breaking Down the Business Plan

estimates can be derived from primary and secondary research. Primary research involves sampling customer pools in an attempt to estimate the level of demand in given areas and among specific customer groups. You can estimate your future revenue by estimating the revenue derived from acquiring a given percentage of the target market. You will want to be very conservative when making these estimations. Secondary research involves identifying the past sales figures and growth rates of similar or competitive products. You will want to document this research thoroughly in order to justify your projections to potential investors.

Investors generally require that an entrepreneur develop three sets of sales forecasts: conservative, expected, and optimistic. While you will focus on the expected sales figures, your potential investors will focus on the conservative figures. On a side note, any increase in sales will have to be accompanied by adjustments to other variables, such as cost of production, marketing costs, sales costs, etc. All of these calculations will go into business financials.

Promotional Budget

How much money are you setting aside for marketing? This question depends on the funds available in your budget after completing other essential activities in starting the business.

Above you outlined the tools or tactics that you plan to employ in communicating your marketing message and your expected sales revenue at a given price. In most cases, you will not have adequate funds to fully employ all of these tools. As a result, you have to prioritize the funds that you spend on your promotion efforts. Traditional marketing methods tend to be more expensive, but can have better results for specific customer markets. Emerging marketing methods, on the other hand, can be far less expensive, but

Breaking Down the Business Plan

fail to reach large portions of the target or available markets. In either case, it is difficult to calculate or determine the most cost-efficient and effective promotion method.

When determining which types of marketing methods to use, do some primary research on competitors or like business. Also conduct some secondary research to determine the medium most likely to reach your target customer market. The results of this research will drive your decision on which marketing methods to employ. Further, it will help you determine how to most effectively allocate your available funds.

Note: Marketing and sales efforts are the life-blood of your business. When allocating funds for marketing, remember that great product or service businesses often fail due to a lack of sales. Even a mediocre business activity will be successful if it can generate sales. In any event, we strongly recommend allocating more money than you initially believe will be required to achieve your projected sales.

Breaking Down the Business Plan

Operational Plan

Overview

The operational plan outlines exactly how your business functions. Generally, the operational plan serves two purposes.

- It allows you to take a holistic approach to your business.

- It provides interested third parties with a description of your business.

More specifically, the operational plan identifies each part, process, or component involved in carrying out your business. The primary components of the business operations plan include:

- a description of the production or service delivery process,

- the business location,

- personnel

- inventory

- Suppliers, and

- payment processing (credit policies and accounts receivable/payable).

You will describe each of these sections in detail to the extent that it is relevant or applicable to your business. You will need to outline where you are in the creation of your business. Specifically, you will explain what steps you have taken to put your business in motion.

Breaking Down the Business Plan

- *Note*: We highly recommend using a flow chart, diagram, or infographic to display the overall process.

Product or Service Development

This section of the business plan regards how you (will) make your product or carry out your service. Here you will outline the day-to-day activities necessary to carry out your business. Start with an outline of all of the processes involved in delivering value to your customers. You will need to account for the necessary production or development activity at each stage in the value chain.

The following are several relevant portions of the product or service development plan that correspond most closely to a product business.

- *Production Process* or *How Services are Carried Out*: Here you will outline the process of manufacturing your product. If you provide a service, you should outline all of the moving parts and individuals necessary to carry out the service. Provide a general checklist or flowchart for delivering value.

- *Production Timeline*: Explain how long it takes to produce a unit and when you'll be able to start producing your product or service. Include factors that may affect the time frame of production and how you'll deal with potential problems, such as rush orders.

- *Production Feasibility*: You will want to give an overview of any research or testing you have done to prove the feasibility of producing your product in accordance with your operational plans. Research could include market research, questionnaires, competitor process analysis, alpha and beta testing of the product, etc.

- *Vulnerability*: You should identify any potential problems that could arise in the production process. Specifically address what flaws in the production or service delivery process could potentially affect the business negatively and how you will handle any such issues.

- *Quality Control*: How will you maintain oversight of the production or service provision process? Develop a plan for supervision of each stage of the process. Remember, it does not have to be you who supervises the process; rather, it should simply be someone who is accountable to you.

- *Customer Service*: What is your plan for customer service? This includes sales communication, return products, and customer follow-up. This component is critical, as customer service is often the last interaction a customer has with your business in a given transaction. Following through with the customer's expectations of your business is paramount. Repeat customers and positive word-of-mouth may be critical to your business's success.

Equipment and Other Assets

In this section, you will address all of the equipment and supplies necessary to carry out the business. Further, you will assess your current assets and your needs, broken down by priority of need, prices, and financing options. This portion is most important for manufacturing or product-based businesses.

Breaking Down the Business Plan

- *Necessary Equipment*: What equipment do you need to carry out the basic operations? What are the costs and purchase/finance options?

- *Current Assets*: You may already have some of the necessary equipment to carry out operations. Identify these assets, and explain what asset requirements they fulfill.

- *Equipment Priority*: Some equipment may be desirable but may not an absolute necessity. Ascribe a level of priority to each piece of equipment. The priority should be higher depending upon the likelihood of the equipment to increase production or efficiency. It may also be helpful to outline the equipment output, required maintenance/repair, and expected life of each piece.

- *Equipment Pricing*: Outline a projected cost for purchasing (new or used) and renting the necessary equipment. You need to explain your rationale for your decision. Don't forget to include a general schedule of maintenance costs for the equipment.

- *Equipment Financing*: Explain any financing arrangements or terms of financing. Make a list of your assets, such as land, buildings, inventory, furniture, equipment and vehicles. Include legal descriptions and the worth of each asset. Identify any equipment or assets that are subject to security interests. (It is important to understand the priority of security interests when multiple lenders claim an interest in the individual assets.)

Special Requirements

Are there any special requirements or situational factors necessary for carrying on your business? In this section you

Breaking Down the Business Plan

will list any requirements that are unique to your business and would fall outside general expectations. This could include special assets, economic conditions, legal or regulatory conditions, etc.

- *Example*: You run a business that sells products in the United States that are manufactured in a foreign country. You work with an importer to bring these goods into the United States. At some point in the process, it could become illegal or heavily regulated to import these goods. You will need to have an alternative-manufacturing plan in place to preserve your business operations in the event of such a legal or regulatory change.

Location

The location of the various components of your business operations is an important consideration in planning purposes. Below are several questions you should answer in this section of the business plan.

- *Location Requirements*: What qualities do you need in a location?

    - *Importance of Location*: Explain the significance, if any, of each physical location to your business. For example, your location may require that you have access to a railroad line, airport, major highway, waterway, etc.

    - *Zoning*: Make certain the anticipated activity meets the applicable zoning requirements. If not, explain a plan to request a variance or petition the municipality for re-zoning.

    - *Power and other Utilities*: What will be your specific power needs. Have estimates for the cost of power and the resources/regulatory approvals necessary to obtain such funding. A strong plan will discuss preliminary data and on-going discussions with the available utility providers.

- *Access*: What type of access do you need to your location? Detail how customers, employees, logistics personnel, etc., will access your business. Ex. Do you need easy walk-in access? Is it convenient for customers and suppliers?

- *Hours of Operation*: Indicate and give a justification for your intended hours of operation. Does your location support these hours of operation? Does it conflict with other local or resident businesses?

- *Physical Buildings*: Describe the type of physical location you require. That is, what attributes must the edifice, business grounds, access roads, etc., have in order to carry out operations. You may have multiple locations or locations designed with specific purposes, such as manufacturing, administrative office, and sales locations. Make certain that you account for the intended growth of your business in your building projections. If applicable, your plan should include the following building specifications.

    - Number of rooms, offices, space utilization, etc.

    - Cost per square-foot

    - Materials

    - Exterior and interior design or layout

Breaking Down the Business Plan

- Parking requirements
- Public access
- Any items additional requirements relevant to growth

- *Value Projections*:
  - *Value*: What is the expected value of the land or buildings required for your business operations?
  - *Rent vs. Purchase vs. Construction*: In this section, you will outline the type of building need or the class of facility. Give an explanation of why this type of building or facility is necessary and how it will fit or accommodate your growth projections. You will also need to justify your decision to rent, buy, or construct. If you plan on undertaking a combination of these activities, justify you decision and how this fits into your business growth plans.
  - *Costs*: Determine a preliminary figure for costs associated with building/occupying the intended location. Examples of expenses include: rent/mortgage, maintenance, utilities, property taxes, insurance, construction/remodeling, etc. These numbers will become part of your financial plan.

Personnel

In this section, you will provide an overview of the key personnel involved in the business and the different jobs or

Breaking Down the Business Plan

positions that will be necessary. Basically, you are going to tell who will do what. Describe whether you intend to hire new personnel or contract with independent contractors to carry out business functions. You will need to account for the personnel requirements as the business grows.

- *Note*: Don't assume that you will need employees for a particular function.

The following are considerations for the personnel section of the operational plan.

- *Startup Team*: Who is part of your startup team? What will be their primary areas of responsibility? Describe what you understand their roles and duties to be, and explain how they are qualified or competent to carry out these duties.

- *Types of Personnel*: Give a general description of the main employees or positions that you will need to fill. This includes skilled, unskilled, and professional employees. As part of this process, you will outline who performs the specific task at each stage of operations. Some of these positions may be filled by independent contractors who render services on a fee-for-service basis. If so, document the nature of these anticipated relationships. At first there will only be a few positions. Try to determine the personnel that will be needed at each stage of the business's growth.

- *Number of Employees*: Construct a timeline depicting the growth in number of personnel in accordance with the projected business growth.

- *Procedural Protocol*: Begin by describing the procedures necessary to effectively carry out each position or function of the business. This is necessary to maintain operational stability as well as consistency in operations. This could include procedural steps or written manuals for carrying out individual stages of the operations.

- *Methods for Recruiting Employees*: You will need to have a plan for recruiting new service providers and skilled professionals. This section is important for professional service or technology companies. Finding the skilled labor necessary to carry out operations in these types of businesses is often very difficult. (*Note*: A good place to start is documented any established relationship with local universities with technical programs and professional schools.)

- *Personnel Training*: How will you conduct training? What will be your plan for preparing new employees? Do you have a continuation plan in the event you lose a key employee? Be careful not to place too much operational importance on any single individual without developing a training plan for replacements.

- *Compensation*: Along with the description of personnel and timeline for employment, you will want to associate an estimated cost at each period in time. As such, you will need to devise a projected compensation structure for employees. It is important to develop a realistic plan that fits the company's revenue projections and incentivizes employees to perform and remain with the business. The startup team or key leadership compensation (including benefits and equity options) is often the most difficult to structure.

Inventory & Materials

In this section you will indicate from where you are going to receive your inventory or the materials necessary to produce your product or carry out your service. You should indicate

Breaking Down the Business Plan

your suppliers or manufacturers and outline the nature or terms of any agreement(s) in place.

- *Inventory*: What type of inventory (finished product, supplies, raw materials, etc.) will you keep on hand and where will you get it?

- *Cost or Value of Inventory*: You will need to use the projections for cost of inventory in your financial projections. A key provision in the pre-money valuation (pre-equity funding) of your business may involve an accurate assessment of the value of assets, including inventory.

- *Inventory Turnover*: (Product businesses) At what rate will you need to restock your inventory? This is an important figure used in assessing the sales strength of the business. You will want to make a special note about how the inventory turnover compares to industry averages.

- *Special Inventory Requirements*: You will also want to outline a plan for dealing with special inventory requirements, such as seasonal fluctuations. This includes a plan for lead-time ordering to be able to meet fluctuations in demand.

- *Inventory Control*: You should establish a plan for monitoring and controlling inventory. This should be incorporated into a employee/personnel description. There are many systems and software applications that make managing inventory much easier. Many of these programs are integrated into the major accounting or bookkeeping software(s).

- *Production Costs*: You will use all of the above information to create an estimate of production costs. Basically, ever aspect of operations will have a cost associated with it. These costs will be split into fixed and variable costs and will be included in your financial projections. As such, you may want to maintain separate figures regarding the cost of goods and the cost of labor. You may also want to categorize production costs for non-recurring and incidental costs associated with operations.

Suppliers

The suppliers section provides detailed information about the companies that will supply you with the inventory or materials outlined above.

- *Supplier Background*: You should include background information on the supplier(s). This information lends credibility to the stability or dependability of his or her service.

- *Inventory Details*: Attribute the type, amount, and cost of inventory supplied by each supplier. We recommend using a table appended to the business plan to demonstrate this information. The written portion should include a summary of this information and a description of any anticipated fluctuations in the requirements or costs of the inventory.

- *Payment Terms*: Outline the terms of performance in the supplier-purchaser relationship. For example: What are the terms of payment? Is there an interest rate or late fee associated? What are the terms of delivery (time period, location, frequency, etc.)?

- *Back-Up Plan*: It is important to have a back-up plan in the event you lose a supplier or the supplier is unable to meet operational needs. This portion will likely include a plan for working with alternative suppliers.

Breaking Down the Business Plan

Having such a plan avoids the danger of placing too much operational importance on a single, third party.

Payment Policies

In this section, you will outline your business's payment terms for the goods or services sold.

- *Issuing Credit*: Are you planning on accepting in-house credit? What will be the terms of payment for customers who purchase on account? You will want to look at industry standards and the payment policies of your competitors. Do not forget that your payment policies can be a point of differentiation between you and those competitors.

- *Determining Who Can Purchase on Credit*: You should have established policies in place to determine who can purchase on credit and under what terms. Remember, you will have to comply with applicable laws, such as the lending laws and the laws prohibiting discrimination. Also, you will have to comply with state and federal regulations regarding background checks.

- *Terms of Credit*: What will be the terms of payment? If you extend credit you will need to decide on the terms of repayment and the interest, if any, attributable to extending the credit. What will be the rate of interest charged and penalties for late payment? Will there be a discount for early payment? (For example, $100 10%, net 30, means $100 is due in 30 days, but if you pay before 30 days you receive a 10% discount or $10 off.)

- *Security Interests*: Will you take a security interest in the goods sold? (Security interests allow you the ability to reclaim the property sold if the debt is not

Breaking Down the Business Plan

paid.) If so, do you have a plan or procedure for documenting these transactions?

- *Slow-Paying or Non-Paying Customers*: You will need a policy for dealing with slow-paying customers. What process will you establish for reminding, urging, and possibly threatening customers to render payment? You should outline an escalating plan for requesting payment, such as making a phone call, sending a letter, using a collection agency, and hiring a collection attorney.

- *Credit Cards*: If you accept commercial credit, do you have a service provider to process the payment? What types of credit will you accept? Will you offer a discount for paying in cash?

- *Costs of Extending Credit*: Any time that you extend credit there is a cost involved. The cost could be the risk of the purchaser not paying, or it could be cost of capital over the credit period. In any event, you will need to build these costs into your financials. For example, there always needs to be some allowance for bad accounts. We recommend estimating a percentage of the accounts that will not be paid.

- *Managing Your Accounts Payable*: As part of the operations process, you may be in the role of creditor to a servicer or supplier. You should develop a plan for payment of accounts owed. The key considerations in developing a payment plan include: maintaining positive relations with the supplier or servicer and optimizing the use of available cash (extending credit as long as possible). If the supplier or servicer offers a discount for early payment, then you should consider whether this option is in your best interest. If your business would greatly benefit from making payment

Breaking Down the Business Plan

toward the end of the available period, then it may be worth extending the payment obligation.

Legal Environment

Establishing and maintaining operations will require the crossing of numerous legal hurdles. You should describe any anticipated legal issues in advance and outline a plan for addressing them. Below are some sample, but common, legal issues.

- *Entity Selection and Formation*: Outline your justification for choosing a given entity structure. Explanations should include: taxation, equity funding, and ownership and control.

- *Business License, Professional Licenses, Inspections, and Zoning Requirements*: Identify all of the licensing requirements for carrying on your business. This includes the licensing of your business, personnel, property, etc.

- *Insurance and Bonding Requirement*s: Outline the requirement for bonding or professional insurance. You should indicate your intentions for obtaining coverage and the cost of such coverage.

- *Permits*: State and local governments require special permits for specific types of business activity. You must conduct the necessary background research on the licensing requirements for carrying on your business in a given area and provide a synopsis of how you will handle those requirements. For example, you maybe a contractor that performs work in multiple states or counties. If necessary, how will you go about obtaining a work permit to carry on your services in the area?

Breaking Down the Business Plan

- *Workplace and Environmental Regulations*: Outline a plan for the necessary workplace inspections and standards. The regulations vary depending on the type of activity you carry on at your business location. These standards can drastically affect your construction plans and applicable costs. Environmental regulations include proper documentation and accountability for waste, environmental surveys of the location, etc.

- *Securities Regulations*: If you intend to sell an ownership interest in your business to outside investors, then you will have to comply with federal and state securities laws. You will need to be familiar with the major provisions and the particular registration exemptions available to small equity offerings.

- *Employment Laws*: Develop a plan for legal compliance with all employment laws. This includes outlining procedures for hiring and firing employees, employee benefits (health insurance, retirement accounts, etc.), worker's compensation, affirmative action (if you accept federal contracts), etc.

- *Taxation*: You will need to identify all of the taxation requirements for your business activity. Types of taxation considerations include: federal tax registration, state tax registration, estimated tax payments, employee payroll withholdings, sales tax registration and withholding, property tax, etc.

- *Protecting Intellectual Property*: You will need to develop a plan for protecting and maintaining all applicable forms of intellectual property, including: trade secrets, trademarks, copyrights, and patents. In some cases, protecting your intellectual property can

Breaking Down the Business Plan

be very costly (such as patent filings). Account for these costs within the financials.

Learning Point

After working through this business plan section, you will have a detailed operating plan and a comprehensive outline of what actions need to be taken next in developing the business. You should maintain the operations plan as a separate document from the overall business plan. Business operations can change rapidly. Keeping the operations plan separate will allow you to effectively use the document for planning everyday operations.

Management Team and Business Organization

Overview

This section regards how your company is organized and who are the primary members of your business team. You will describe how your business will be managed and who will be involved. This includes developing a plan for the roles of individual members. While individual member roles and responsibilities often change rapidly, you want to have a formalized chain of authority within the business. Remember, too many decision-makers and no single person with authority can be a major challenge to the success of a business.

- *Note*: Laying out the title and role of individuals concerns your type of business organization.

Business Management

This section should include the names, positions, and general biography of the key business personnel. Outside business investors (angels or venture capitalists) who are assessing your business will want to know all about the level of experience and qualifications of the management team. At a bare minimum, you should include answers to the following questions.

- *Name*: Who are the key individuals involved in the management of your business?

- *Title*: What will be those individuals' titles?

- *Responsibilities*: What primary responsibilities does that position entail?

- *Qualifications*: What are their background and qualifications for carrying out their intended responsibilities? This will include work experience, educational degrees, and prior experience in startup ventures.

Organizational Chart

We recommend that you create a formalized flow-chart demonstrating the hierarchy of authority within the business. If the chart is large, you can add it to the appendix. This organizational chart should be cross-laid with the core operational responsibilities of the business. For example, you may split the business responsibilities into the following sections.

- Operations

- Sales & Marketing

- Administration & Governance

Outlining the business in this fashion will give individuals a clear sense of their responsibilities. Further, it will establish formal chains of authority that will become increasingly important as the business grows.

As you add new employees, you will want to integrate them within the organizational chart. Make clear the chain of authority and reporting. Outline both the responsibilities of each individual and their authority to represent the interests of the business. Your plan will gradually become more and more specific about the roles and responsibilities of individual members. You may also consider developing a plan for cross-training individuals for specific tasks. You don't want your business to hinge or become dependent solely upon the presence of a single individual.

Breaking Down the Business Plan

This chart will also serve as credentials for business when approaching outside investors. These investors will want to see that the business is stable and that there is ample talent to perform all of the functions necessary to carry out the business's functions and growth goals.

Professional and Advisory Support

When forming your business, you will begin to forge relationships with outside parties who can provide advice and services to your business. Depending on your business organization, you may have professional advisors, such as a board of directors, or you may have a less formal advisory board. Below is a list and explanation of some of the more common professional and advisory support for a startup business.

- *Accountant* - An accountant can be extremely valuable in 3 areas: Entity formation, business compliance, and tax strategy. An accountant will be able to help you understand the tax considerations that go into choosing an entity type. One can also help you understand the rules for business compliance, state and federal income tax, tax deductions, tax credits, sales & use, transfer, deductions, capital gain loss, employee withholding, estimated tax payments, financial statements, auditing, etc.

- *Small Business Attorney* - A small business attorney is useful in a number of important areas. Entity selection and formation, contracts, financing or equity arrangements, intellectual property, employment law, securities regulation, business compliance & governance, collection efforts, etc.

- *Insurance Agent* - Depending on the nature of business, you may require various types of insurance coverage. Common types of insurance include casualty

Breaking Down the Business Plan

& damage on property, personal injury protection, professional liability, life insurance, health insurance in employee benefit plans, etc.

- *Banker* - We cannot express the importance of having a relationship with your bank representative. Many small businesses make the mistake of banking with large financial institutions, rather than choosing smaller, more intimate, local banks. When you are seeking loans to operate your business you will have a much easier time working with a banker who knows you personally and understands your business.

- *Mentors* - Find someone who you know and respect to serve as your mentor. Preferably, this is someone who has experience with startup ventures. Starting a venture can be nerve-racking. It helps to have someone offering guidance who has gone through this process before. This person will provide moral support as well as expertise in a particular industry.

- *Board of Advisors* - A board of advisors is similar to a semi-formal group of business mentors. Rather than providing moral support, these individuals help to guide you through the process of starting, managing, and growing your business. You should try to assemble a diverse group with a variety of professional experience. Preferably, these individuals will be a mix of knowledgeable entrepreneurs and industry experts.

- *Board of Directors* - If you choose the corporate form to do business, you will have a board of directors. Many closely held corporations do not have outside members on the board of directors; rather, the board consists of the owners and key members. As the business begins to grow, you may have directors who are either equity investors or experts who you

Breaking Down the Business Plan

compensate with equity ownership. In either case, you should seek investors and experts who can provide the greatest degree of guidance and support to your business.

You will want to detail the names, experience, and qualifications of these individuals within the Management and Organization section. The primary purpose is to demonstrate to outside investors that you have adequate support to handle your operations and intended growth path.

Learning Point

A business is only as strong as its individual members. How these members interact in support of the business activity is extremely important in creating value for the end customer and in assuring the growth and prosperity of the business.

Financial Projections

Overview

Financial statements are backwards-looking summaries of the financial performance of the business. Financial projections ("financials"), on the other hand, use the same documents to look forward and project the performance of the business. Because these projections have not yet happened, drafting the financials is more of an art than a science. You want to be optimistic about the potential performance of your business, yet you need to remain realistic at the same time.

- *Note*: Visit www.TheBusinessProfessor.com for links to free templates of business financial projections.

The financial projections ("financials") portion of the business plan may be surprisingly unique depending on the business. As previously discussed, the business plan serves two primary functions:

- use by owners or managers in planning the business, and

- obtaining business financing through loans and investment capital.

Developing the financials section will give the business founder or managers a plan for budgeting, estimating future expenses and revenues, and business projections. Likewise, a lender or outside investor will depend greatly upon the financials in evaluating the appeal or risk of investing in the business.

The primary pieces of the business financial projections including the following sections.

Breaking Down the Business Plan

- Assumptions

- Income Statement

- Cash Flow Statement

- Balance Sheet

- Financial Calculations Sheet (Optional)

Below we go through multiple sections of the business plan that meet the above purposes.

Note: Depending on the use of the business plan, it may be advisable to remove certain sections for a specific purpose. For example, when presenting the business plan to equity investors, it may be advisable to remove the portion regarding the financial status of the founders. Likewise, as the business develops the financial condition of the owners may be less relevant than the corporate fiscal health.

Assumptions

Assumptions provide the building blocks of the financials. They detail the individual assumptions regarding the sources of revenue, the startup expenses, the required working capital, and the fixed and variable costs of operations. The following are the categories of assumptions you will need to develop. Each assumption should have its own page.

- *Startup Cost Assumptions*: In this section you lay out all of the costs that you will incur in starting up the business. Startup presumptions are further broken down into the costs of fixed assets and the working capital necessary to finance immediate operations.

    - *Fixed Startup Costs* – This section regards the upfront expenditure necessary to begin

Breaking Down the Business Plan

business. This section generally includes the cost of physical assets that have some sort of long-term value (buildings, equipment, etc.).

- Here you will want to state all of the fixed assets that must be purchased for the business. If the assets are rented, then include any down payments or other initial outlays of cash necessary to begin business. The monthly rent payments will be allocated later to fixed expenses in the income statement. Some assets will have a useful life of more than one year. In this case you will depreciate the asset over a set number of years for tax purposes, but you will record the initial outlay of cash in the startup costs. Below are examples of the type of fixed startup costs you may incur.

  - Building: $5000 down payment + 1st month's payment on financing
  - Renovations: $15,000
  - Truck: $3000 down payment + 1st month's payment on financing
  - Equipment $8000 + 1st month's payment on financing

- *Working Capital* – Money that will be used to finance short-term operation of the business such as deposits, insurance, and advertising, until the revenue from the business are sufficient to sustain operations. Most businesses will lose money early in the life of the business. You will need sufficient funds to sustain the business (and potentially yourself) during this time. Eventually, the business will reach a break-even point and be self-sustaining. Until

Breaking Down the Business Plan

the business produces sufficient revenue to cover its operating expenses, the business will have to rely on working capital to fund operations.

- Generally, you will complete the working capital section after completing the income statement. The income statement will show you the amount of revenue, expenses, and profit or loss that you sustain each month. It will also indicate at what point your business reaches break even.

- Add up the projected losses of each month (from the income statement) until the business reaches break even. Now, double that amount. Then add in the total fixed startup costs. The final amount is a good estimation of your required working capital.

- Working capital generally comes from the equity that owners place into the business, business loans, or outside equity investors. See the financing assumptions below.

- *Financing Assumptions (Sources of Money)* - Where are you going to get the money to move forward with the business? How much money will you get? What will the terms of the money be (i.e., the interest rate on the money)? Generally, the primary methods of financing include: owner's Injection of capital; proceeds from bank or other loans; debt from an owner or outside creditor; and equity capital from an investor. These funds will have to be sufficient to cover the startup costs (fixed startup costs and working capital).

Breaking Down the Business Plan

- *Note*: In the introduction of this section of the business plan, you may wish to disclose the personal net worth, assets, obligations, outside investments, and sources of income of each individual. This information can be rather personal, but it serves multiple purposes. Demonstrating the financial status of the founders, owners, or major stockholders gives an indication of the ability of these individuals to supply necessary capital to the business. The partners, members, shareholders, etc., will have more confidence if the other owners have the financial ability to meet the capital needs of the business. This information serves the dual purpose of satisfying the requirements of lenders and investors. Potential investors will want assurance about the owner's ability to meet the financial needs of the business. Likewise, lenders will take the resources of these individuals into consideration when making the determination of whether to extend credit. Unless the company has considerable assets to post as collateral, lenders will require founders/owners to sign personal guarantees for the debts of the business.

- *Fixed Expense Assumptions* - In this section, you will outline the cost of being in business. Take a look at the operational plan. Try and identify all of the expenses that you will incur on a monthly basis in carrying on operations. These include payment of rent, mortgage payment, utility expenses, wages of full-time employees, insurance, etc. The key aspect in identifying an expense as a fixed (versus variable) expense is that you will incur the expense regardless of how much product or service you sell. In the

Breaking Down the Business Plan

startup expense section, you identified fixed asset expenses. Many of these items will be financed and will become a fixed expense.

- *Variable Expense Assumptions* - These are the expenses that you will incur with unit of product or service sold. That is, the costs are present or accumulate with the number of sales. Take a look at the operations plan, and identify every operational activity that will cost money but only arises pursuant to the sale of an item. Examples of variable expenses include inventory, parts, raw material, fuel, sales commission, etc. The reason you want to calculate these expenses separately is because you need to calculate variable costs as a percentage of revenue. This will allow you to approximate your variable costs easily as revenue fluctuates.

  - *Example*: Your revenue per item sold is $10. Your variable expenses are $5 per item. You variable expenses as a percentage of sales is 50%. If you have revenue of $1000, then you can estimate your variable expenses as $500. You don't have to calculate each individual variable cost, as this would be difficult and time consuming.

  - *Note*: Your revenue should always be sufficient to cover variable expenses (as variable expenses only relate to individual products sold or services rendered). Otherwise, your business loses money with every item sold or client served. In the beginning, however, your revenue may not be sufficient to cover variable expenses and fixed expenses. In the meantime, you will cover these expenses with working capital. Once you reach the point where

Breaking Down the Business Plan

revenue covers fixed and variable costs, you have reached break even.

- *Projected Revenue Assumptions* - This lays out the potential sources of revenue and how much you will bring in from each source. A business may have multiple sources of revenue that are either fixed (such as return on investment assets held or government allocations) or variable (revenue from monthly sales). In this section, you will draw from your marketing research to estimate expected volume of sales and average price of goods or services sold.

  - *Example*: Multiply the price of your good or value per hour of service x the projected number of products sold or hours billed. Over a month, this will be part of your revenue projection for that month. Add up all of the income from the various sources of revenue and you have your monthly revenue projections.

  - *Note*: Be realistic in your revenue projections. Researching competitors or similar businesses can provide you with a good understanding of the volume of customers or clients to expect in a given month.

- *Cash Flow Assumptions* - This simple statement regards the payment terms. If you sell products or service on credit, then you will have to account for the period of time it takes for customers to pay their invoice. This is usually based on a percentage of payments over 30, 60, and 90 days. You will take your expected revenues and adjust them for payment terms for customers or clients. Likewise, you will adjust some of your variable expenses to indicate at what point you will actually make payment for the

Breaking Down the Business Plan

parts, raw material, etc., used in carrying on your business.

- *Note*: Poor cash flow planning is a top reason for businesses failing. The problem lies in that they poorly plan their use of cash and cannot meet their payment obligations.

Now, let's use the information we outlined in the assumptions to build the financials.

The Income Statement

The income statement, also known as the profit and loss statement, combines the revenues and expenses of your business. The profit and loss projections include all sources of revenue (including the capital contributions of owners) and all costs/expenses associated with the business.

Most financial projections expand the income statement out for three years. The first year is broken down by months for all twelve months. The second and third years are broken down either quarterly or annually.

The income statement is broken down as follows:

- *Revenues*: The first section demonstrates all sources of revenue from business operations. You can draw this information from your projected revenue assumptions. Your sales revenue will be the expected price x the projected number of goods sold in any given month. Other revenue (not a part of regular business revenue) will be listed in the income statement at the time they are received.

- *Variable Expenses*: The next portion should include the variable expenses of operations. These are your costs of goods sold or service-based expenses.

Breaking Down the Business Plan

Remember, we calculated variable expenses as a percentage of sales. This makes it easy to calculate the variable expenses for each month. Simply take your variable expenses as a percentage of sale (50% in the above example) and multiply that percentage by the total revenue from sales in the given period (e.g., month). This will provide a calculation for the costs of producing the goods or services.

- *Fixed Expenses*: The next section includes the fixed monthly costs. Here you will give a breakdown of all costs and expenses of startup and operations, including the cost of capital (i.e., interest on loans). Again, you will draw this information from your assumptions. Include the startup costs in the early months when incurred. The fixed expenses will continue for each consecutive period and may increase as production increases. That is, the fixed expenses generally increase with the purchase of more assets, the growth of the business operations, or economic conditions that change the prices of set resources (such as fuel or electricity).

    - *Note:* You should allocate a percentage of any contingency funds (funds spent on unexpected expenses) to miscellaneous expenses during the 12-month period.

Here are some general tips about the income statement.

- Profit/Loss projections should be laid out month-by-month for the twelve-month period. Basically, you will subtract fixed and variable expenses from your revenue during each month. This will produce either a profit or loss in the beginning.

    - *Note*: Profit projections should be accompanied by a narrative explaining the major assumptions

Breaking Down the Business Plan

used to estimate company income and expenses.

- The 12-month projections should be as detailed as possible. The revenue portion will generally be very simple in comparison to the expenses portion. The important point about the revenue portion is to make certain that your revenue projections are realistic. Too many business plans over-estimate revenue from sales early in the startup's life. Remember, the number one reason why businesses fail is a lack of sales. This leads to inevitable cash flow problems.

- Now that you have a 12-month plan, you should start working on your 3-year financial projections. The 3-Year projections should contain all of the same elements as the 12-month projections. There should also be additional elements to the revenue section to account for increased sales, new infusions of equity, or additional debt. The expenses section must account for the projected growth in cost of goods sold (if applicable), personnel expenses, cost of capital, etc.

- The 3-year financial projection serves two purposes:

    - a strategic and financial planning tool for the founders, and

    - the business proposal to potential investors.

At this point, it is important to remember the difference between a small business and a startup venture. The small business hopes to exist, grow, and provide a continued livelihood or employment for the owners. Startup ventures are growth-based projects. The entrepreneur, along with any investors, looks to capitalize upon sale or exit of the business venture. Investors in the business will want to see a detail 3-5 year projection showing the intended growth path of the

Breaking Down the Business Plan

business. The growth of the business (i.e., the increased revenue) will be the metric by which the sale price is determined. The sale price gives the investor a target rate of return on their investment.

Projected Cash Flow

Cash flow is generally considered the absolute most important component of business operations. Statistically, poor cash flow management is a leading cause of business failure. An interesting statistic is that more than one half of the business declaring bankruptcy in 2012 were profitable on their income statements. The reason they faced bankruptcy was attributable to poor planning for the use of cash. These businesses were unable to meet present obligations due to a delay in receiving payments from customers or the misuse of cash on other aspects of the business causing a shortage when needed.

- *Note*: This is why having a sizable line of credit is essential to business operations. Businesses that have large fixed expenses, such as wages and salary, can draw upon the line of credit when needed. Many small businesses suffered or failed during the past few years due to the cancellation of lines of credit caused by the economic recession.

The cash flow projections allow you to visualize the movement of money in and out of your business. Planning the use of cash is critical in the budgeting process.

You can think of the cash flow statement as your checkbook. You start out with an amount in your bank account (owner's contribution, loans, equity investment, retained earning, etc.). Each month you begin with the previous month's balance and add in any new sources of revenue and capital. The amount of cash inflow each month is based off of your revenue projections and financing assumptions. The

Breaking Down the Business Plan

beginning cash balance will be adjusted each month, based upon the actual result of cash flow for the prior month. As for expenses, you will subtract from the cash balance any costs or expenses actually paid in the month.

- *Note*: The above explanation brings up an important point. Depreciation and amortization are not really expenses that you pay in a given month; rather, they are accounting adjustments. So, you will only subtract amounts from the cash balance where you actually transfer cash out of the business.

To summarize, the cash flow statement breaks down the revenue and expense component of the financial projections into individual transactions over a stated time period. You will define individual sources and amount of revenue on a week-by-week or month-by-month basis. Remember, the cash flow projections deal with the period in which money comes in and goes out. Just because goods are bought or sold in a given month, that does not mean that cash changes hands.

You should record every transaction based on the actual receipt or amount paid at the time of payment. These projections should be updated weekly, as the amount of payments made may vary throughout the week or month. Further, your expenses projection should be based on the same time period as the revenue projection, so that you can easily compare the two.

- *Note*: Business revenue tends to vary more than expenses. Revenue is based upon sales projections, which are subject to the whim of the consumers. Many of the organization's expenses are fixed. For example, think about rent payments or payroll expenses. These payments will remain constant each week or month. Variable expenses, such as materials associated with sales or other incidentals will vary along with sales.

Breaking Down the Business Plan

Try to use any prior historical references you can to estimate these amounts.

Your underlying purpose of the cash flow projections is to actively plan for the allocation of resources throughout the year. You certainly do not want to have a cash deficit, but you equally do not want to have an extreme surplus of unused cash. A deficit can ruin the business, while a surplus indicates inefficient use of funds.

The Balance Sheet

The balance sheet is a snapshot of your business at a given point in time. It consists of your business's assets, liabilities, and owner's equity (i.e., equity invested by owners + earnings retained in the business). It is often difficult to account for the retained earnings at a given point. Many entrepreneurs just think of owner's equity as simply the assets (or asset value) minus the total liabilities of the business. The importance of this document is that it gives an overview of company's overall solvency.

You will begin your balance sheet by accounting for all of the assets of the business. You will categorize these assets into broad categories for accounting purposes, such as cash, equipment, real estate, inventory, investment assets, prepaid expenses (such as insurance or rent), etc. You will want to break these assets into current assets (i.e., assets that are easily converted to cash) and long-term assets (which are far less liquid). It is not likely that you will have too many categories of assets at the very beginning.

On the liabilities side, you will outline all of the obligations of the business. You can look back on your expenses calculations to re-check all of your existing liabilities. Like the assets, you should categorize the liabilities by grouping them into short-term and long-term liabilities. For example,

Breaking Down the Business Plan

the accounts payable would be a short-term liability, where the mortgage obligation would be a long-term liability.

The owner's equity will equal the difference between the value of assets and amount of liabilities. This amount can be far different from the actual amount invested in the business plus the amount of retained earnings. The reason is due to capital appreciation/depreciation of assets and any losses suffered by the business.

While the balance sheet generally provides a snapshot of the business at a given point in time, you may want to develop an end-of-year projected balance sheet. When you are presenting your financial projections to a lender, she may want to see a projected balance sheet in order to understand the collateral and obligations that will exist at a future date. You will make these projections from your expected growth path. If you plan to reinvest cash flow to purchase additional equipment, then you would adjust your assets and owner's equity accordingly. Likewise, if your growth path calls for increasing your debt or accounts payable, then you can project this in your accounts payable.

Financial Calculation Sheet

Outside investors in your business will want to know the business' ability to produce a return on their investment. Below are the calculations that you should include within your business plan that demonstrate the business' financial progress.

Break-Even Analysis

A break-even analysis is a projection demonstrating the level of sales at which you break even. This statement takes into account the total expenses of the business for a given time period (week, month, year). There are a number of ways to

Breaking Down the Business Plan

arrange the formula to calculate the break-even point. Here is a basic formula:

- Your Total Costs (TC) have to equal your Total Revenue (TR); TC =TR

    - *Note*: In your projections, the total revenue from sales will equal the total costs of sales, including fixed and variable costs.

    - *Note*: Your Total Costs (TC) equals your Fixed Costs (FC) plus Variable Costs (VC): TC = FC + VC

    - *Note*: Total Revenue (TR) equals Avg. Price (P) times the Number of items Sold (N); TR = P x N

Calculate the fixed cost associated with doing business during this time. When the Total Revenue from sales equals the Total Cost of operations for that period, that is your break-even point. You previously calculated your total fixed costs for a month. These do not vary considerably each period unless you purchase more equipment or hire more people. Your variable costs change depending on the amount of resources used to produce and sell the product or service. These calculations are taken from your original expense calculations.

Now, given the price of the good or service (or average price of a combination of good and service), what is the volume of sales (N) that you will need to achieve this revenue break-even point? You can figure this out by solving for (N).

$$N = TC / P$$

If the total cost to make your goods is $500 and the price is $5, then you need to produce and sell 100 goods to break even.

Breaking Down the Business Plan

Payback Period

Remember, one of the key purposes of the business plan is to attract lenders and investors. One calculation that either financier will want to see is the payback period for money provided. The payback period is simply the amount of time that it takes for the financier to regain her total investment. The common formula for calculating payback is:

- Payback = Initial investment / Cash Inflow per Period (Amount of money paid out to Investor).

The only problem with this formula is that it assumes that there is a positive cash flow at the end of each period and that the cash inflows are consistently the same amount. The best way to demonstrate payback is to add the total profits estimated to accrue after reaching the break-even point. When the total profits equals the amount invested, then this is the lender/investor's payback point. Now, in reality the lender or investor will not be paid back during this period. The payback period simply indicates the period of time in which the business could feasibly pay back the loaned or invested funds if desired.

Internal Rate of Return

The internal rate of return is a more complicated calculation. The calculation itself is not complicated, but the significance is somewhat complicated. The rate of return is generally calculated as:

- (Capital Invested - Capital Returned) / (Capital Invested) = Rate of Return (Express as a percentage, so multiply by 100%).

    - *Example*: If you invest $100 in Capital and you receive a Return at the end of the year of $50,

Breaking Down the Business Plan

then your Rate of Return = ($100 - $50) / ($100) = 50%.

This calculation is fairly simple, but it can be more complicated. A lender loans money at a rate of interest. That rate of interest is the rate of return. An equity investor however, generally loans money without any terms of repayment. The investment purchases equity in the business. In some cases the equity investor will want to continue to own the portion of the business and receive a distribution of the earnings each year (called a dividend). If this is the case, then the investor will only invest if they believe that she will receive a certain dividend amount each year. This is the investor's internal rate of return year-over-year.

More often, however, the equity investor will seek to recoup her investment at some point in the future (usually 3-10 years) at some exit event. The exit event could be the sale of the business, going public with the business, or simply selling the equity back to the business or to some other third-party investor. In this situation, the investor will be curious about what her rate of return over the life of their ownership will be. Remember, the equity investor is investing money and taking the risk of the business failing. If the business fails, the investor generally loses all of her money. If the assets of the business are sold, the lenders or debt holders get paid back first. This situation causes lots of risk for the equity investor. As such, the investor will wish to receive a very high rate of return for the risk incurred.

Equity Investment Summary

Equity investment is a topic for another text, but here is a brief overview:

The equity investor invests money with an expected return on investment at a future date (e.g., sale of the business in 5 years). In order to take on the risk involved in this investment, the investor will calculate an expected rate of return. For example, an early angel investor may seek a 100% return on investment year-over-year. So, to determine whether she will achieve this mark, she calculates the value of the business at the projected sale date and determines how much of the business she will need to own at that time. So if the business needs $100,000 of investment, the equity investor will need a return of $500,000 in five years at the time of sale. If, after looking at the financial statement and similar transactions of similar types of businesses, the investor calculates that the business will be worth $5 million in 5 years, then she will want to purchase 10% of the business with the $100,000 investment.

This situation gets increasingly complicated as you learn about valuing a business, the dilution of equity ownership, and other factors affecting the investor's rate of return. In any event, the investor will look at your investment and be curious about the rate of return that she could possibly receive from the investment. This amount will be important when negotiating the amount of equity interest that the investor will receive in exchange for her investment.

Learning Point

Investing significant time in calculating realistic financial calculations will serve as an excellent tool for planning and financing the business. Along with the Executive Summary and Management Team, the financial projections are the most important variables in attracting lenders and investors.

Breaking Down the Business Plan

The Appendix

Overview

The appendix is where you place material that adds to the business plan but does not fit neatly or belong in the body of the plan. Generally, the appendix is used to include exemplars of material or information that is referenced within the business plan. You can include any outside information necessary to support the propositions or assumptions within the business plan.

Examples of Appendix Material

Consider including the following information or materials in the appendix of the business plan.

- *Marketing Material (Advertising)* - The ability to drive sales is a critical part of the business plan. Providing samples of marketing material can help provide an understanding of the brand that you are attempting to build around your product or service.

- *Primary and Secondary Research* - In order to effectively market your product (and establish a brand) you have to understand your target market. Further, you will need market estimates in order to accurately evaluate the market potential and potential profit from pursuing the venture. This material should support the figures that you introduce within the business plan.

- *Designs or Property Layout Material* - Perhaps you have designs, artwork, facility plans, etc., that provide a picture of your intended venture location, buildings, image. This can help third parties to understand your vision.

Breaking Down the Business Plan

- *Important Contracts* - Providing proof of key contracts (such as leases, supplier contracts, etc.) adds substance to otherwise seemingly hypothetical plans. Again, this will provide comfort to potential third-party investors.

- *List of Key Assets* - Providing a list of key assets within the business plan would be too large and cumbersome. While you will include the collective value of the assets within the financial section of the business plan, it may be a good idea to attach an itemized index for review. This can help in the budget planning process.

- *Organization Chart and Employee Backgrounds* - Within the business plan you provide a concise background of your employees and an organizational chart. Here, you can provide a more in-depth background on your key employees and their curriculum vitae. If you have other key employees, you may want to provide their backgrounds, key roles, and responsibilities.

- *Customer or Expert Endorsements* - Customer or expert endorsements can serve as excellent credibility for your product or service. While you may mention these or provide brief quotations within the business plan body, it is often a good idea to include the whole endorsement or letter within the appendix.

Learning Point

All of the above material can be instrumental in planning the business. Also, outside lenders or investors may feel greater confidence if they have this additional information. Caution - Do not overload the business plan appendix with unnecessary material. Include things that you definitely believe add value to the planning and business assessment process.

Breaking Down the Business Plan

Finalizing The Business Plan

This text outlines the major sections and the general information included within the business plan. Depending on the use of the business plan and the nature of the business, you will develop separate versions of your plan for specific purposes. Continue to focus on the purpose of your business plan, use it as a planning device, and continually update the plan as your business progresses. You will make modifications to the plan to meet immediate objectives and long-term plans.

Throughout the text, we focus on the planning purpose of the business plan. We also me make reference to the use of the business plan to attract investors or to satisfy lenders. Below are summaries of the specific purposes of the business plan.

Obtain a Loan

A lender will want to understand the risk associated with making a loan. Besides making the borrower sign a personal guarantee for the loan, the lender will closely review the business plan details. The lender will focus on:

- the estimates for revenue and expenses (with an eye for the potential of your idea to become a stable and operating business), and

- the hard assets of the business (to serve as collateral for the loan).

Below are some aspects of the business plan to show additional attention for this purpose:

- *Loan Amount*: How well is the amount borrowed explained or justified within the business plan? You will need to be specific and provide a line-item summary of the intended purposes of the funds. The loan officer will look closely at the financials to determine whether the projected capital needs are consistent with the loan amount.

- *Priority of Funds*: What is the spending priority for the funds? How will each intended expenditure relate to the key purposes of the business? The loan officer will want to see how these funds will strengthen the business.

- *Re-Payment Terms*: You will need to have an understanding of how a similar business loan is structured. What interest rate can you expect, and what is your proposed plan for repaying the loan? Of course, the lender will structure any approved loan, but you should understand the key provisions of the type of loan you are requesting. This will help your ability to negotiate the payment schedule or length of repayment.

- *Security Interest*: The lender will look to understand the level of security in the loan. Aside from the success of the business, the primary consideration of the lender will be the available collateral to secure the loan. You will have to provide assurance that the lender will have a security interest with priority in the collateral or after-acquired property.

Attract Investors

Investors seek to invest in or acquire an interest in a high-growth company that will provide a high return-on-investment at a future exit event. The investor will seek a rate of return commensurate with the level of risk in the investment. Risk encompasses the probability that the business will fail or not meet its intended growth. Below are

Breaking Down the Business Plan

some aspects of the business plan to show additional attention for this purpose:

- *Use of Funds*: The investor will do a close inspection of the financials to determine the intended use of funds. She will focus closely on:

    □ the amount needed up front,

    □ the rate of expected spending, and

    □ the ability of the funds to meet the immediate business needs.

- *Sufficiency of Funds*: Will the funds be sufficient to meet the expected growth of the business? Is the investor intending to provide multiple rounds of funding? If no, will the investor's equity be diluted with future equity rounds? If the investor will not make future investments, do you have a plan for future equity rounds?

- *Financial Calculation*: You will want to make certain that your financial projections meet the intended interest of the investor. Explain the percentage of equity offered and the offered price. The intended equity price must meet the investor's desired rate of return. Further, you will want to explain the intended rights and provisions associated with the equity. For example, account for the anti-dilution rights of the investor or the right to participate in future equity offerings. There are numerous conditions that you will have to consider in the financing arrangement. Do your research and address these issues in the proposed equity offering.

- *Exit Strategy*: What is the intended exit strategy?

Breaking Down the Business Plan

- ▫ *Example*: Sell the business to a strategic purchaser (a firm with compatible operations); sell to a private equity firm (or competitor); owner buyback (generally as a leveraged buy-out), sale of equity to the public (an initial public offering). How long until you reach the exit strategy? Is there a backup strategy? This should be constructed as a worst-case scenario to quantify the risk involved.

- *Investor Involvement*: What level of involvement or control will the investor exert? Will the investor seek a role in management, on the board, serve as a strategic advisor, or be completely hands off? You will want to account for the investor's expectations and your willingness to allow investor involvement.

Updating the Business Plan

Overview

The business plan should be a living, growing, evolving document. Each section of the business plan can be its own document. You should feel free to add additional details and modify the plan to meet your purpose. As the business proceeds through its life cycle many of the projections, expectations, and plans will change. It is important to modify the plan accordingly and maintain its utility as a planning instrument. Below is a rough outline of the life cycle of a business with the business plan overlaid.

www.ingramcontent.com/pod-product-compliance
Lightning Source LLC
Chambersburg PA
CBHW051731170526
45167CB00002B/887